Earthquakes

Neil Morris

CRABTREE PUBLISHING COMPANY

www.crabtreebooks.com

The Wonders of our World

Crabtree Publishing Company

PMB 16A	612 Welland Ave.,	73 Lime Walk
350 Fifth Ave.,	St. Catharines,	Headington
Suite 3308	Ontario, Canada	Oxford OX3 7AD
N.Y., N.Y. 10118	L2M 5V6	United Kingdom

Author: Neil Morris
Managing editor: Jackie Fortey
Editors: Penny Clarke and Greg Nickles
Designer: Richard Rowan
Art director: Chris Legee
Picture research: Robert Francis

Picture Credits:
Artists: David Ashby 9, 10, 15; John Hutchison 24;
Janos Marffy 4, 12, 20; Ann Savage 14.
Maps: AND Map Graphics Ltd.
Photographs: Colorific! cover, title page, 13, 18, 19 (bottom);
Robert Francis 7 (bottom), 8 (bottom); Gamma 17 (bottom), 22-23, 23;
Robert Harding Picture Library 5, 20, 26, 26-27; Hutchison Library
12-13, 28, 28-29, 29 (top); Caroline Jones 21 (bottom);
Pictor International 24-25; Popperfoto 11 (bottom), 19 (top);
Science Photo Library 6, 7 (top), 10, 11 (top), 14, 15, 16-17, 21 (top),
22 (bottom), 27; Stock Market Photo Agency 4-5, 8-9, 29 (bottom);
Topham Picture Point 3, 16 (bottom), 17 (top), 25.

Cataloging-in-publication data

Morris, Neil
    Earthquakes / Neil Morris.
    p. cm. — (Wonders of our world)
Includes index.
ISBN 0-86505-832-6 (library bound) ISBN 0-86505-844-X (pbk.)
Summary: Discusses what an earthquake is, some major
earthquakes in history, how quakes impact humans, and the
science of measuring and predicting these disasters.

1. Earthquakes—Juvenile literature. [1. Earthquakes.] I. Title.
II. Series: Morris, Neil. Wonders of our world.
QE521.3.M65 1998   j551.22   LC 98-3306 CIP

CONTENTS

WHAT IS AN EARTHQUAKE?

A N EARTHQUAKE is a sudden shaking of the ground caused by movements beneath the earth's surface, or crust. The crust is made up of huge rocks called plates. The plates slowly move and rub against one another, causing pressure to build below the surface. When the pressure becomes too much, the plates jolt past each other, sending out the shock waves that produce an earthquake.

Small earthquakes simply make the ground tremble. Big ones can cause the earth's crust to crack, buildings to collapse, and people to die.

MOVING PLATES

Some of the biggest quakes occur where one plate is forced under another (below). The lower plate grinds against the upper plate.

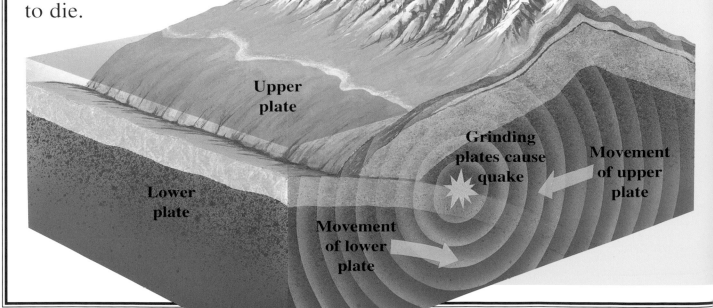

Upper plate

Lower plate

Movement of lower plate

Grinding plates cause quake

Movement of upper plate

DAMAGE AND DESTRUCTION

These houses (left) in San Francisco, USA, were almost destroyed by an earthquake in 1989. During the quake, the ground shook for fifteen seconds. More than 24,000 houses were damaged and 63 people were killed. Most earthquake deaths are caused by fires, landslides, and falling buildings.

ROCK LAYERS

The earth's plates are made up of rock layers called strata. If these strata are bent so much that they finally break, they form a crack called a fault. This photo (right) shows the line, or crack, of a small fault running diagonally through layers of limestone and shale. The block of rock to the left of the fault line has slipped down.

WHERE IN THE WORLD?

EARTHQUAKES OCCUR all over the world. There are thousands of minor quakes every year. Most are small tremors that cause little damage. Each year, however, there are some larger, more damaging earthquakes. Most take place in one of two zones.

About three-quarters of the world's earthquakes occur in a zone around the Pacific Ocean. This zone is known as the "Ring of Fire," because it has many active volcanoes. The other zone runs from Southeast Asia through the Middle East to the Mediterranean Sea.

EARTHQUAKE ZONES

Both main earthquake zones occur along the edges of plates.

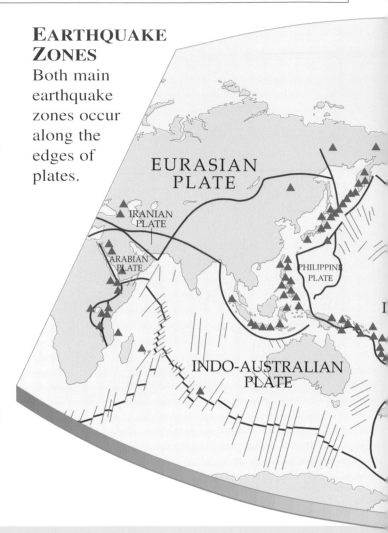

EURASIAN PLATE

IRANIAN PLATE

ARABIAN PLATE

PHILIPPINE PLATE

INDO-AUSTRALIAN PLATE

LISABONA

PORTUGAL, 1755

This engraving (left) shows the earthquake in Lisbon, the capital of Portugal, on November 1, 1755. Huge waves swept through the harbor. On land, buildings collapsed and fires broke out. More than 60,000 people lost their lives and the city was destroyed.

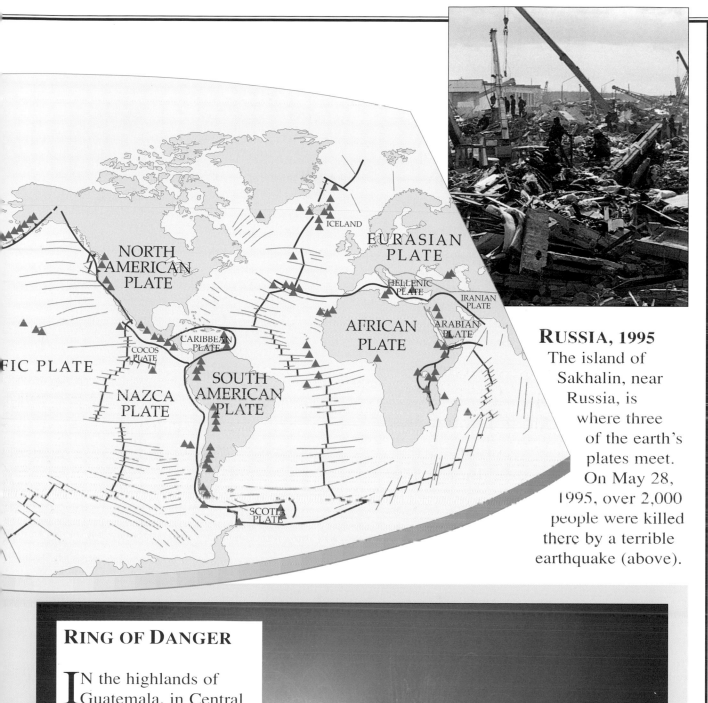

NORTH
AMERICAN
PLATE

ICELAND

EURASIAN
PLATE

HELLENIC
PLATE

IRANIAN
PLATE

AFRICAN
PLATE

ARABIAN
PLATE

CARIBBEAN
PLATE

COCOS
PLATE

FIC PLATE

NAZCA
PLATE

SOUTH
AMERICAN
PLATE

SCOTIA
PLATE

RUSSIA, 1995

The island of Sakhalin, near Russia, is where three of the earth's plates meet. On May 28, 1995, over 2,000 people were killed there by a terrible earthquake (above).

RING OF DANGER

IN the highlands of Guatemala, in Central America, a chain of 33 volcanoes overlooks the coastal plain. Volcano Pacaya is one of them. The region suffers many earthquakes, such as in 1976, when 23,000 people died and over a million lost their homes.

MOVING FAULTS

T HE SURFACE of the earth is full of faults. Faults are cracks in the earth's crust, where rocks have broken under the huge forces created by moving plates. Many faults are large enough that they have split open the ground.

The lines these cracks create are called fault lines. Large fault lines may go into rocks deep underground and stretch along a whole continent. The world's biggest fault lines, and strongest earthquakes, are found near the edges of the earth's plates.

FAULT PLANE

Blocks of rock scrape past each other along fault lines. In a normal fault, one block of rock slips down, exposing the fault plane of another block (see the diagram on page 9). The picture below shows a normal fault plane in the Severn Valley, in England. It was exposed by earth movements which took place millions of years ago.

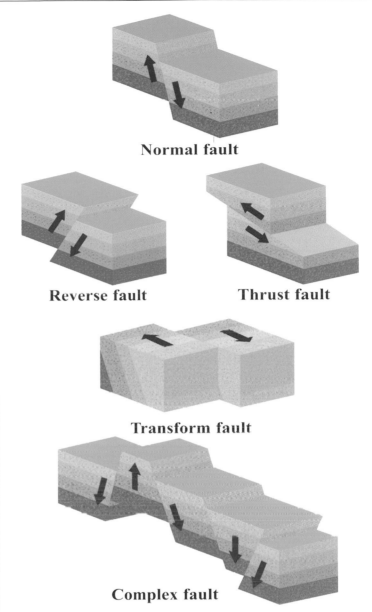

Normal fault

Reverse fault

Thrust fault

Transform fault

Complex fault

DIFFERENT TYPES OF FAULTS

A NORMAL fault is usually caused when rocks are pulled apart and one block slips down. If rocks are pushed together, they may create a reverse or thrust fault. In these faults, one block is forced up and over another block. Transform faults, which are also called strike-slip faults, form when blocks of rock, or even whole plates, slide past each other. Sometimes a series of neighboring faults forces rocks to move in many directions, forming a complex fault.

SPLIT OPEN

There are many sizes of faults. Lines range from just a few inches (centimeters) to hundreds of miles (kilometers) in length. The large fault line above is exposed, or has left an open split in the ground. Such splits can occur anywhere along any kind of fault line.

SAN ANDREAS FAULT

CALIFORNIA, USA, has had many big earthquakes. They happen because the Pacific coast of California is along the San Andreas Fault. This transform fault is 750 miles (1 200 kilometers) long and is on the boundary between the Pacific and North American plates. These two plates slide past each other at the rate of about 2 inches (5 centimeters) each year. Smaller fault lines also cross the area, and cause thousands of tremors in California every year.

FAULT LINE

The San Andreas Fault runs across the Carrizo Plain (above), about 100 miles (160 km) north of Los Angeles. The city itself is located to the west of the fault (see the map, left), but San Francisco is almost on the fault. As the ocean plate slides north, the land plate moves south.

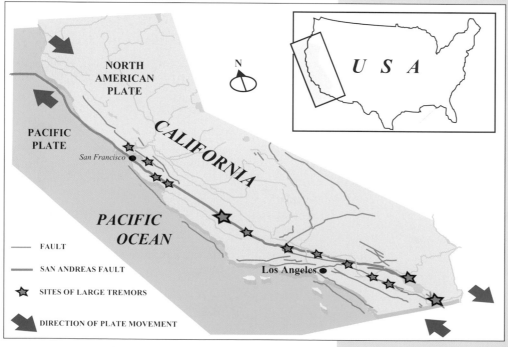

NORTH AMERICAN PLATE

PACIFIC PLATE

San Francisco

CALIFORNIA

PACIFIC OCEAN

N

U S A

Los Angeles

— FAULT

— SAN ANDREAS FAULT

☆ SITES OF LARGE TREMORS

➤ DIRECTION OF PLATE MOVEMENT

SAN FRANCISCO

FIRES burned in San Francisco after the 1906 quake (right). Plate movements along the San Andreas Fault caused the disaster. The city shook for one minute. At least 3,000 people were killed and 28,000 buildings destroyed.

LOS ANGELES

Although Los Angeles, the second largest city in the USA, is not right on the San Andreas Fault, it too is in an earthquake zone. On January 17, 1994, the city was struck by an earthquake which killed 60 people and left 25,000 homeless. The shaking knocked down ten highway bridges and closed three major freeways. The earthquake was the result of a smaller fault which thrust the ground upward at the community of Northridge.

SHOCK WAVES

EARTHQUAKES MAY begin as far as 435 miles (700 kilometers) below the ground. The focus, or hypocenter, of the earthquake is where rocks first jolt. Vibrations called seismic waves, or shock waves, move out from the focus. The waves travel at up to 10 miles (16 km) a second through the ground. The point on the earth's surface above the focus, called the epicenter, is where the shaking is strongest. As the shock waves travel away from the focus, they get weaker.

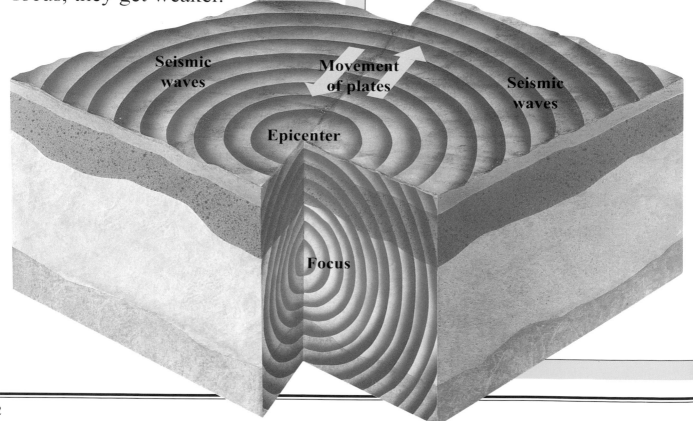

Seismic waves

Movement of plates

Seismic waves

Epicenter

Focus

FORESHOCKS AND AFTERSHOCKS

Foreshocks and aftershocks are tremors felt before or after the main quake. The Japanese people above are sheltering in case aftershocks cause more destruction.

FARAWAY DESTRUCTION

Mexico City suffered a terrible earthquake in 1985 (left). The quake's epicenter, however, was 220 miles (350 kilometers) away, on the Pacific coast.

WAVE TYPES

DIFFERENT types of seismic waves move out from a quake's focus (left). Body waves (right) travel either as straight P waves or as snake-like S waves. At the surface (far right), they are either Rayleigh waves, which move like sea waves, or Love waves, which move with a side-to-side motion.

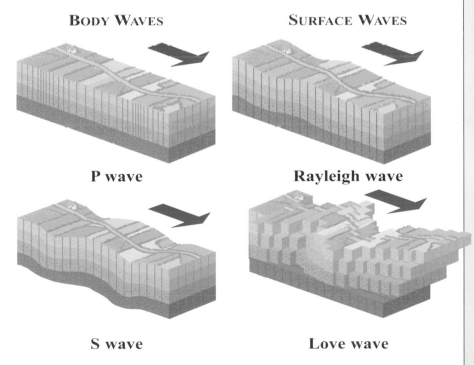

BODY WAVES

P wave

S wave

SURFACE WAVES

Rayleigh wave

Love wave

MEASURING TREMORS

SEISMOLOGISTS ARE scientists who study earthquakes. They measure ground movements with a seismograph. Seismographs around the world are linked so that seismologists can share information and locate a quake's focus and epicenter. The strength of a quake's movement can be shown as a number on a scale. The best-known scale is the Richter scale, but today, other scales are also used to measure the strength of an earthquake.

SEISMOGRAPHS AND SEISMOGRAMS

Seismographs (above) measure ground movements. Then they make lines on graphs, called seismograms. Seismograms are printed on computer screens or paper, and show an earthquake's strength.

AN ANCIENT SEISMOGRAPH

THIS seismograph (left) was invented in China around AD 130. Earth tremors cause a pendulum inside the pot to swing, forcing one of the dragons to drop a ball into a frog's mouth. The dragon that drops the ball points out the direction of the tremor.

USING LASER BEAMS

Lasers are used to accurately measure the tiniest ground movements. This laser station (above), in California, USA, gives precise information about the many small tremors that happen there all the time. Laser beams are aimed at a series of reflectors on the other side of fault lines. This system can pick up movements of less than 0.04 inch (1 millimeter).

MEASURING EARTHQUAKES

IN 1902, Giuseppe Mercalli invented the first scale to measure earthquake damage. In 1935, Charles Richter created a different system. Richter's system was based on the strength of seismic waves. Each increase of one on the Richter scale means a 10-times increase in the strength of an earthquake.

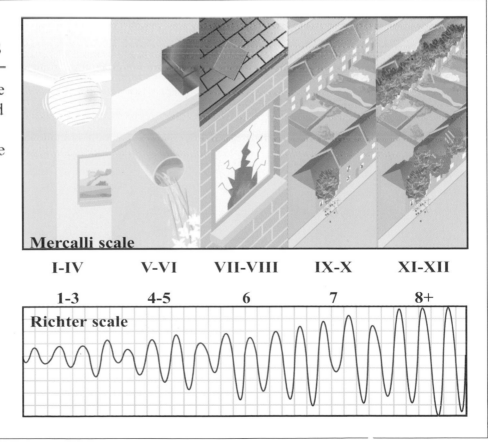

Mercalli scale

| I-IV | V-VI | VII-VIII | IX-X | XI-XII |

| 1-3 | 4-5 | 6 | 7 | 8+ |

Richter scale

BIGGEST QUAKES

EARTHQUAKES HAVE happened regularly throughout earth's history. They have always done damage to buildings. Four of the famous Seven Wonders of the ancient world, for example, were destroyed by earthquakes. Worse still, quakes have claimed millions of human lives. The worst earthquake tragedy in history, in China in AD 1556, killed 830,000 people. People in the past knew little about the cause of earthquakes, which probably made these disasters even more frightening to them.

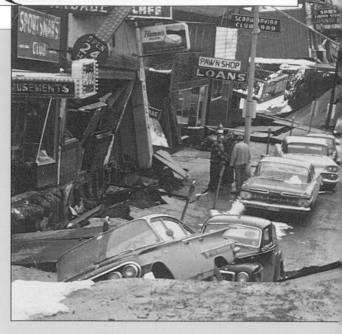

ANCHORAGE, ALASKA, USA
On March 27, 1964, an earthquake measuring 8.4 on the Richter scale tore apart the main street in Anchorage, Alaska (above). The quake started a landslide that destroyed many other Alaskan towns and killed 131 people.

TOKYO, JAPAN

ON September 1, 1923, the ground shook for five minutes in Tokyo and the surrounding areas (left), as the nearby Sagami Bay Fault cracked. Thousands of buildings collapsed and fires broke out. More than 100,000 people died.

ROUDHON, IRAN

Thousands of people in Roudhon, Iran, died and many more lost their homes as whole towns and villages were destroyed in 1990 (below). On the Richter scale, the earthquake measured 7.3.

VALDIVIA, CHILE

IN 1960, an earthquake caused a town in Valdivia, Chile, to sink almost 7 feet (2 meters). The quake measured 8.3 on the Richter scale. It was one of the strongest ever recorded. It also caused the eruption of a new volcano (above).

DISASTER!

AT 5:46 a.m. on January 17, 1995, disaster struck Kobe, Japan. This industrial port lies on the coast of Japan's largest island, Honshu. Japan itself is situated where four of the earth's plates meet, and suffers many small earthquakes every year. The 1995 quake killed 5,500 people and damaged 190,000 buildings. It was twice as strong as the quake that hit Northridge, California, on exactly the same day, one year earlier.

WATER PROBLEMS

The Kobe quake broke water mains and hindered firefighters. Water was cut off from nearly a million homes, and people stood in line for small supplies.

LIVING OUTDOORS

THE quake shut off gas and electricity and left most buildings unsafe. People felt nervous about staying in them, and many moved outdoors. Some inhabitants of Kobe, such as the man shown left, wore a mask to keep from breathing in dust and germs.

SHAKEN TO THE GROUND

The Kobe earthquake turned an elevated section of the Hanshin Expressway on its side near the city center (above). This demonstrated the terrible strength of the earthquake. Its epicenter was about 10 miles (16 kilometers) away from Kobe, beneath the Akashi Strait that separates Honshu from Awaji Island. The focus was 10 miles (16 kilometers) beneath the sea bed.

OLD AND NEW

MANY old buildings in Kobe were destroyed (right), especially those with heavy tiled roofs and weak wooden walls. Most were just one or two stories tall. Some of the city's newer, much taller buildings survived because they had been built with earthquakes in mind. Amazingly, many of these skyscrapers were damaged at the bottom, while the upper floors escaped without damage.

PLANNING AND BUILDING

SEISMOLOGISTS AND engineers have learned many lessons from disasters in Japan, the USA, and elsewhere. Seismologists now have a better idea of which areas are likely to have earthquakes. Planners know where to build, and engineers have designed structures to withstand some quakes. Bolting buildings to foundations and strengthening their walls with reinforced concrete or steel beams are two new building methods.

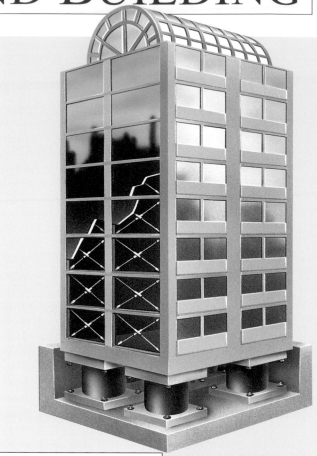

HIGH-RISE TOKYO

JAPANESE architects and builders have developed new building methods for the skyscrapers of Tokyo (left) and other cities. They still fear, however, that it is impossible to make a building that will stand up to a giant earthquake.

RESISTING EARTHQUAKES

Some earthquake-resistant buildings have rubber and steel pads, called isolators, at their base (above). The isolators act as shock absorbers, and the space around them lets the building sway without collapsing. Walls of reinforced concrete may be strengthened with steel beams.

TESTING STRUCTURES

ENGINEERS use special vibrating machines to test scale models of new structures. They produce the same effects as an earthquake. This machine (left) is being used to test a nuclear reactor.

TRANSAMERICA PYRAMID

This unusual skyscraper (right) is San Francisco's tallest building, at 853 feet (260 meters) high. It was specially designed to withstand earthquakes.

QUAKE WATCH

SCIENTISTS WORK to find new ways of predicting when and where earthquakes will occur. They put special equipment in high-risk areas. Strainmeters and creepmeters measure tiny movements along fault lines, and tiltmeters show changes in ground slope.

These devices help warn people who live in danger zones that a big tremor might occur. When they receive these warnings, people must be ready to take precautions very quickly.

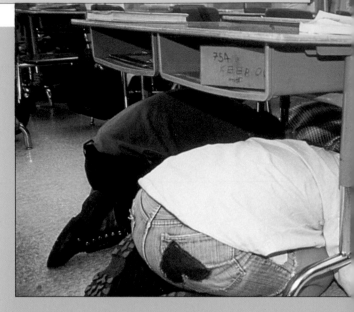

EARTHQUAKE DRILL

These schoolchildren (above), in Los Angeles, USA, are used to earthquake drills. If they are indoors when shaking starts, they must shelter under a desk.

PREDICTING TREMORS

IN California, USA, scientists use many methods to try to predict tremors. In the experiment shown left, equipment in 18 wells measures groundwater levels. Data is transmitted to a seismographic station for checking. Any sudden changes could mean that the ground is moving.

SURVIVAL KIT

HOMES and offices in earthquake zones can be equipped with special survival kits. These kits contain supplies that could help people stay alive after an earthquake, especially if the people are not found for a long time. The kits must be stored where survivors can find them in seconds.

TRAVELING EXHIBITION

This exhibition in Japan (below) prepares people for the frightening experience of an earthquake. The model room shakes and shudders.

TSUNAMIS

EARTHQUAKES THAT happen in rocks beneath the ocean can cause huge waves. These waves are called tsunamis, from the Japanese words for "harbor waves". Tsunamis, which can reach heights of more than 98 feet (30 meters), bring destruction to harbors and built-up coasts. These giants are sometimes called "tidal waves," but they have nothing to do with tides.

In the open ocean, a tsunami can move at 500 miles (800 kilometers) an hour. The quake in Chile in 1960 (see page 17) caused a tsunami that swept across the Pacific and struck Hawaii 15 hours later, with waves 39 feet (12 meters) high.

WAVES BUILDING UP

UNLIKE waves made by the wind, tsunamis affect water right down to the ocean floor (below). Out in the deep, open ocean, a speeding tsunami is normally 8 to 12 inches (20 to 30 centimeters) high. As the tsunami reaches shallower water near the shore, its waves slow down and bank up to their greatest height. Huge waves can pound the shore for many hours.

Waves hit shoreline

Shock waves

Epicenter

OKUSHIRI ISLAND

THE island of Okushiri lies off the west coast of northern Japan. On July 12, 1993, Okushiri was hit by a tsunami caused by earthquakes beneath the floor of the Sea of Japan. The biggest quake measured 7.9 on the Richter scale and its epicenter was 80 miles (50 kilometers) offshore. The tsunami caused destruction (above) and killed 192 people.

LANDSLIDES AND MUDFLOWS

IN MOUNTAINOUS areas, earthquakes can set off landslides. If rocks and soil are not stable, slight earthquakes far away can shake them free. Once this happens, the material, sometimes together with ice and snow, flows downhill and engulfs everything in its way.

Such a slide is what happened on Mount Huascaran, the highest peak in the Andes, in Peru, on May 31, 1970. An earthquake off the Peruvian coast, beneath the Pacific Ocean, shook the mountain and caused a landslide that buried a town.

YUNGAY, PERU
This bus (below) was caught in and battered by the landslide from Mount Huascaran. The town of Yungay, Peru, completely disappeared. Over 50,000 people were killed.

RAIN AND MUD

Heavy rain can cause rock, loosened by earthquakes, to collapse. Rainwater makes rock and mud heavier, increasing the likelihood of a landslide or mudflow. Landslides such as this one in the Himalayas (left) often happen after some small tremors and rain.

ALASKAN LANDSLIDE

THE Alaskan earthquake of 1964 (see page 16) also caused massive landslides. Many houses had been built on loose rock and soil, and they were carried along on the landslide before being smashed to pieces. The quake also caused a tsunami, which struck the coast of Alaska with waves over 16 feet (5 meters) high. The tsunami reached as far south as California.

TODAY AND TOMORROW

EARTHQUAKES ARE a natural part of the way our planet works. They show the immense forces that continue to shape the world.

We cannot stop earthquakes, but we can continue to learn about them in the hope of saving human lives. In the future, scientists may invent instruments to monitor the earth's plates from deep underground or from space satellites, orbiting the earth. With this technology, we may become better at predicting when and where earthquakes will next strike.

CLOSE CALL

WHEN the Hoover Dam (left) was built in the USA in 1936, the weight of water in its reservoir set off strong tremors. Fortunately the dam did not collapse, and engineers learned useful lessons from this and other dam projects.

OLD BUILDINGS . . .

Armenia (left) lies between Europe and Asia. In 1988, an earthquake made 500,000 Armenians homeless. The buildings could not withstand earthquakes. It took years to rebuild them.

. . . AND NEW

In Japan, new buildings (right) are designed with earthquakes in mind. Damage is quickly repaired.

SEISMOLOGY

THE science of seismology will continue to help us learn more about the causes of earthquakes. Seismologists take information from all over the world. They use computer programs to find out what might happen during future earthquakes.

29

GLOSSARY

Aftershock   A small tremor after an earthquake

Body wave   A seismic wave that travels deep underground

Complex fault   A series of cracks in which blocks of rock move in many directions

Creepmeter   An instrument that measures very small ground movements

Crust   The hard outer layer of the earth

Epicenter   The point on the earth's surface directly above an earthquake's focus, where the shaking is strongest

Fault   A fracture, or crack, in the earth's surface

Fault line   The line made by rocks slipping along a fault

Fault plane   The surface of a fault, along which blocks of rock slip

Focus   The place underground where rocks jolt and an earthquake starts

Foreshock   A small tremor before an earthquake

Hypocenter   The focus of an earthquake

Mercalli scale   A scale, created by the Italian seismologist Giuseppe Mercalli, used to describe damage caused by an earthquake

Mudflow   A landslide of mud

Normal fault   A type of fault in which a block of rock slips down

Plate   A huge, slowly moving piece of the earth's crust

Quake   An earthquake

Reservoir   An artificial lake use to collect and store water

Reverse fault	A type of fault in which one block of rock is forced up and over another block.
Richter scale	A scale, created by the American seismologist Charles Richter, that measures the strength of an earthquake
Seismic waves	The shock waves of an earthquake that make the ground shake
Seismogram	A record, made by a seismograph, of an earthquake
Seismograph	An instrument to record the strength and location of earthquakes
Seismologist	A scientist who studies earthquakes
Seismology	The study of earthquakes
Shock wave	A vibration, or shaking movement
Strainmeter	An instrument that measures strain in the earth's crust
Strata	Layers of rock
Strike-slip fault	A transform fault
Surface wave	A seismic wave that travels along the surface of the earth
Thrust fault	A type of reverse fault
Tiltmeter	An instrument that measures very small changes in ground slope
Transform fault	A fault in which blocks of rock slide past each other
Tremor	The shake caused by a small earthquake
Tsunami	A giant ocean wave caused by an earthquake under the ocean bed
Volcano	An opening in the earth's crust through which molten rock comes from deep inside the earth

INDEX

4 5 6 7 8 9 0 Printed in the U.S.A. 7 6 5 4 3 2